SOMERSET
In the Second World War

SOMERSET
In the Second World War

Felicity Hebditch

Somerset Books

First published in 2005 by Halsgrove
© 2005 Felicity Hebditch

Front cover photograph: *A small child at Williton. She is carrying her gas mask
in its box in case poisonous gas was used as it had been in the First World War.*
Back cover illustration: *'Trevor Jones reading the News' by Syd Durston.*

ISBN 0 86183 422 4

British Library Cataloguing-in-Publication-Data
A CIP data record for this book is available from the British Library

SOMERSET BOOKS
Somerset Books is a partnership between
DAA Halsgrove Ltd and Somerset County Council
(Directorate of Culture and Heritage)
www.somerset.gov.uk

Halsgrove House
Lower Moor Way
Tiverton EX16 6SS
T: 01884 243242
F: 01884 243325
www.halsgrove.com

Printed and bound by The Cromwell Press, Trowbridge

Contents

I
Unwillingly to War

On 3 September, 1939, Britain and France declared war against Germany. Children listened to the broadcast with their parents, or the people they were staying with:

We were called home from our play to sit with our parents and listen to the then Prime Minister, Mr Chamberlain, make his now famous speech that meant we were at war with Germany. My mother cried and my sister cried with her without knowing why. My father was angry and with good reason as he had fought in World War I and had been a prisoner in Germany. (Eric Saffin wrote this about when he was a boy.)

One little boy sat licking his ice-cream and thinking 'Life is really rather good. I wonder what all the fuss is about?' Gradually they were to learn what all the fuss was about. Their lives and everybody's lives changed in a war that was truly a world war.

People in Britain had been expecting war to happen. They could remember the First World War which ended just twenty years before and they didn't want another like that. Hitler planned to make the Germans the 'master race' over a new empire in Europe. He built up the German army to one and a half million men with six panzer (tank) divisions with a new Luftwaffe (airforce) of 2000 planes.

The War Memorial in Vivary Park, Taunton. Perhaps you can find one of your family named on a memorial.

Evacuees arriving at Williton Station. Children came with their school teachers and were chosen by their new foster mother when they arrived.

On Friday, I September 1939, Germany invaded Poland. The government decided that war was definitely going to start and they expected that Hitler would bomb Britain straight away, so they began 'Operation Pied Piper', a plan to take four million children from the towns to keep them safe in the country. Most of them went with their school. Somerset was a safe 'reception area' and people who were willing to take children into their home had given their names months before. Now trains full of children were arriving in the West Country. Edward Baverstock and his school got to Bridgwater in the evening. People came to their doors to see them – this was the first sign for them that the war was really happening.

A girl from Dagenham said they could see their mothers crying when the children boarded a train taking them away …
We all felt very lonely. We didn't know where we were going or what was happening. We were all very tired and bewildered. I went to a farmhouse called Kosy-Kot, with Mr and Mrs V. White. I was parted from my twin brother. He went to farm at Pedwell and I didn't meet him again for over a month.
(*Somerset Within Living Memory*. Somerset Federation of Women's Institutes.)

One girl described Taunton Station when the trains arrived with hundreds of children:

They were met by dozens of helpers; my job was runabout girl. They were taken to Taunton Market. There was a great hush when the first arrivals came into the huge building. Mothers carrying babies, boisterous boys, shy little girls, all with gas masks over their arms and looking bewildered. Gradually during the day places were found for them in Taunton and surrounding villages with kindly householders.

Children who went to Weston-super-Mare had never been to the sea-side before. Living in the country was a surprise too, with no loo indoors and no electricity, but lots of animals.
The girl from Dagenham said:
…I was very happy with the Whites and helped on the farm, feeding the calves, sheep, poultry, geese, ducks and turkeys…I was the only one from our very large London school who stayed in Somerset, and didn't go back after the war except for holidays. …I was married at Orchardleigh. Mrs White treated me like a daughter, and we are still great friends.

Edward Baverstock also came from Dagenham. Edward, aged nine, went with a friend to Shapwick in September 1939. They felt it was an adventure. They had their clothes in a pillowcase and carried a knapsack with things to eat. They woke on their first morning to the sound of sheep and felt themselves in 'a wonderland'. Their foster-parents,

A small child at Williton. She is carrying her gas mask in its box in case poisonous gas was used as it had been in the First World War.

Mr and Mrs Stephens, were so kind. They had two children they played with. In the evening they played board games, and did drawing.

They spent three years on a farm at Shapwick – there was no electricity so they used oil lamps and a range for cooking, or a small paraffin stove in warmer weather. It was a wonderful old house; 'If you looked up the wide chimney you could see the stars at the top.' There were stone flags on the floor. The water came from a pump in an outhouse, where the laundry was done. There was a walk-in larder. The farm had barns, hayricks, cow stalls, a piggery. They made their own cider with the apples from their orchard. The boys herded cows and got to know about sheep and the countryside. It was a fine summer in 1940 and they helped with the hay making and the harvest with Jack the pony. There was plenty of food compared with the rationing at home. Only sugar, jam and tea were short. Edward's parents sent him occasional parcels with clothes as he outgrew his. His parents came to visit once or twice a year. His father loved the farm and helped with the hay making.

When he reached fourteen, school-leaving age, in August 1943, Edward had to leave the village school and returned home with the present of a rabbit in a box. From the train he could see how badly damaged London was. His house seemed very small. He must have missed the family; he still visits them.

Some children went to stay with relatives. Dorothy Evans' parents lived in Birmingham. They brought her and her brother to their grandparents in Beckington. When they arrived, they found that grandma was already looking after two boys from London. (Not many people had phones to ring beforehand.) It was a tiny house, '2 up and 2 down', so grandma, Dorothy and a frail aunt slept in one bedroom, grandpa, two evacuees and her brother in the other. Dorothy remembered how smelly it was. The loo was in a little brick shed in the garden, so at night they used chamber pots. To have a bath, water had to be heated on the stove and put in the tin bath – Dorothy didn't want to have the bath-water after the boys. Dorothy's grandmother was about seventy. She couldn't manage very well with four children to look after. Finally Dorothy's brother was ill so Dorothy wrote home herself and posted it without a stamp. Their parents came and took them home.

Some parents arranged for their children to go to someone kind: Roy Palmer's parents lived in Bristol, a dangerous and noisy place to be, with anti-aircraft guns just outside their house. His parents took him

Children with their teacher at Minehead. Some children had never been to the sea and it seemed like a glorious holiday.

to Butleigh as he was becoming so frightened of the war. He stayed with Mr and Mrs Bush who made him very welcome. He loved country life – Butleigh was still a country village with its wheelwright making carts. 'It was a calm and peaceful time of my life. The war hardly touched Butleigh at all.' His parents paid 10/- (50p) a week for his upkeep. When he went back to Bristol, Mrs Bush had saved all the money and gave it to him.

Many foster parents were really kind and loving to the children. One was adopted when his parents were killed in the Blitz. But some foster parents didn't want to have children in their houses and evacuees ran away. Women in Minehead usually let rooms in summer to paying guests. The government paid 8/- (40p) per week for evacuees' food but it was difficult to provide good meals for that much.

Some evacuees came from very poor families. Somerset people were shocked to see the children had only the clothes they were wearing.

The *Gazette* newspaper reported on the *Kindness of Wellington people to a school evacuated from Bethnal Green. The children could not understand sitting down to a meal at the table, 60% of their food at home was fish and chips. Some were sleeping in a bed for the first time. Some had put on a stone in weight. They had two allotments – most of the children had never gardened before.*

(*Gazette*, 1.3.41)

Seeing for themselves how poor some were made people think that there shouldn't be such a difference between poor and rich.

Parents in the towns wanted to see that their children were happy.
There were lively scenes in the Princes Road Car Park (Wells) on Sunday when the coaches were preparing to return to London with the parents who had come down to the city to spend a few hours with their children. Several parents had made up their minds to take the children home with them, and the kiddies arrived with their luggage which was placed in the coaches but the parents were informed that the children must not return. Mothers and children clung to each other and wept as their baggage was taken from the coaches.

(*Wells Journal*, 13.10.39)

2
Schools

Mostly children went away with their school and school teachers. Children like Roy Palmer and Dorothy and her brother who didn't come with their school found it difficult to fit in. There was teasing over accents and fights in the playground between evacuee 'skinnies' v. Somerset 'swedebashers'. In Glastonbury there were about a thousand extra children to find school places for.

Card game. School teachers were really very different from these funny cartoons. It must have been hard to look after so many children.

Two schools would use one building:
The local children will attend from 8.30 till noon, and the evacuees from 12.30 to 4.30 p.m.

Some children did not stay in one place in the war. They went home when at first the bombing didn't happen. But when bombing attacks started the next summer (July/August 1940), they went back to the safe areas. By 1944 most of the raids were over and some children went home, then new V1 and V2 rocket attacks on London and the South East began again. It was very difficult to have enough schools and teachers but it became even more difficult when people went backwards and forwards and teachers got called up into the Forces. Schools began to have hot dinners for the first time, to help foster-mothers, especially when they were expected to do factory jobs during the day. There was a shortage of books and paper and they couldn't do woodwork lessons because there wasn't enough wood. Schools didn't usually have shelters.

Wire mesh screens to be put over windows in case of flying glass particles, or adhesive tape. Older children to shelter in open country under supervision, or by arrangements with neighbouring householders and with written concurrence of parents and ARP – they need cover within five minutes of leaving their desks.

(Somerset County Council Education
Department instruction to schools)

Huish Primary School was very near Westlands Aircraft factory.
During… 1942, we attended lessons in pupils' homes who lived near the school, taught by mothers and teachers, because of fear of a direct bomb onto the building.

(*Somerset Within Living Memory*. Somerset
Federation of Women's Institutes.)

Wrantage School was bombed. Luckily nobody was hurt as it was during the school holidays. Some boarding schools were sent to grand houses, like the Bishop's Palace in Wells.

3

Others Needing to be 'Safe in Somerset'

Rachel Reckitt in London told her mother she was sending six children, with a nanny to look after them, to her house in West Somerset. Zoos found homes for some of their animals. Rachel Reckitt had a dingo.

Some Jewish refugees came to Somerset. They held the Passover in St Andrew's Church, Taunton.

Big houses and hotels were taken over by the government for various needs. Pixton Park in Dulverton became a nursery for toddlers and expectant mothers. Whole hospitals were moved out of the London area and the cities. Several hundred patients from Park Pruett mental hospital near Basingstoke were moved to Cotford, near Taunton.

Rachel Reckitt's mother embroidered this picture of her house with the six evacuee children at the bottom. Rachel had a dingo from the zoo, which is also on the embroidery.

Evacuees

1.9.39	Operation Pied Piper – children evacuated
	Blackout begins
1.9.39	Germany and Russia invade Poland
3.9.39	Britain declares war on Germany
30.9.39	30% of mothers have gone home
9.12.39	Rebilleting evacuees – Present foster parents feeling the strain
13.9.40	Princess Elizabeth makes her first broadcast, to evacuees
22.5.41	Bristol children arrive in Somerset.
14.6.44	First 'doodle-bugs' – V1 flying bombs – land in Britain
3.7.44	Children evacuated from London again
By 12.7.45	54,317 evacuees had returned to London

4

Fathers

Men had to join the Army, Air Force or Navy unless they were unfit or needed in Britain in a 'reserved occupation' (such as a factory worker or farm worker). More and more were called up. There were five million men in the Forces in 1944/5. The Somerset Light Infantry fought all over the world, in the desert in North Africa, in Italy and India and Burma. Fathers didn't see their children for years. When they came back their children didn't know them.

At first they didn't have enough weapons. Shepton Mallet was a reception area for troops. When the first 1000 men arrived in August 1939, they didn't have uniforms or guns. If you were a Conscientious Objector, not wanting to fight, you were given alternative war work. The Society of Friends do not believe in war so they ran ambulance services.

There were several airfields in Somerset, such as Westonzoyland where RAF planes like Spitfires and Mosquitos went out to fight the Nazi bombers as

Shoe shine for soldiers in Cairo. Some Egyptian boys made a living shining shoes. British soldiers – the 'Desert Rats' – were fighting the Italians and then the Germans in the Desert.

Soldier talking to a girl in the mud in Italy. The Italian dictator Mussolini declared war on Britain but the Italian people did not want a war.

Lorry carrying supplies up mountains in Italy. The British and American armies had to fight in very hard conditions. Although the Italians gave up, the Germans in Italy continued fighting.

The easiest way for the Home Guard to patrol on Exmoor was on horseback.

they came over towards Bristol or Cardiff. At Yeovilton the Navy trained pilots who would fly from aircraft carriers. They came here from places like Canada and Australia and went to fight the Japanese.

Everybody was expected to volunteer for something, Men who were too old or too young to be called up joined the Home Guard, an army of civilians who would fight the Germans if they landed in Britain. The Somerset Home Guard learnt how to shoot in quarries where they couldn't harm anyone. They were expected to capture any Germans whose planes crashed – one took over a milk float to pick up his prisoner! Children were frightened when their father in the Home Guard brought home a German prisoner. They seemed really terrifying.

The Home Guard marching in Yeovil.

Troops

1.5.39	Compulsory military service for men
1.10.39	250,000 men called up for military service
19.12.39	Canadian forces arrive in Britain
1.1.40	2 million men aged 19-27 called up for military service
14.5.40	Local Defence Volunteers (renamed the Home Guard on 23.7.40) founded
4.6.40	Churchill makes a speech 'We will never surrender'
20.6.40	Australian and New Zealand troops arrive in Britain
1942	USA troops in West Country
25.8.42	The King's brother, the Duke of Kent, killed on active service
June, 1944	1,650,000 USA troops in Britain on eve of D-Day
20.11.44	Home Guard disbanded

5
Hitler on the Attack

Was Britain going to be invaded? It seemed quite likely in 1939. If you were a child in Somerset then, you might have seen soldiers busy making defences to keep you safe. On the North Somerset coast powerful guns were set up at Brean Down and Steep Holm to shoot at enemy ships. Big concrete blocks were put on the beaches, and 'awful barbed wire covered the beach where earlier we had played and bathed with such freedom'.

In case an army landed in Devon or Dorset, the 'Taunton Stop Line' was built, a line of pillboxes, small almost-round brick buildings that soldiers could shoot from. Big German tanks could have just pushed on past.

Barrage balloons floated along the edges of targets such as Filton aircraft factories or Westlands, Yeovil and Weston-super-Mare; wires slung in between them could entangle attacking aircraft. There was a balloon hangar at Poulett.

Enemy bombers came at night. Anti-Aircraft guns were set up with searchlights to shoot them down. Eric Saffin and his friends got to know the anti-aircraft gun crew in a field near where they lived: *Searchlights were positioned around the countryside and we had two near Cotford... They had a Nissen hut*

A pillbox on a beach. These small buildings were to protect soldiers firing out to sea if an enemy landed.

Children filling sandbags at Minehead. Important buildings were surrounded by bags of sand to support them if they were shaken by blast from a bomb.

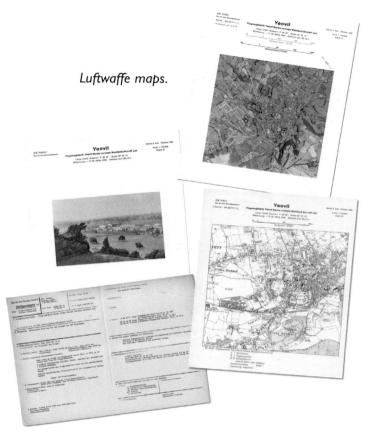

Luftwaffe maps.

where the troops lived and slept and I think there were about eight in the crew. The searchlight and its generator were in an emplacement out in the middle of the field... Searchlights were in use most nights lighting up whole areas as light as day... A dozen or so vast fingers of light would rise from all around and converge at the top of a cone with a tiny moth-like aircraft transfixed in the point at the top. This could be hazardous for the crews as often the enemy planes would fire their machine guns down the beams at the lights below... sometimes planes would drop the odd bomb as well as firing machine guns at them.

Col John Turner who made film sets for Shepperton Film Studios, designed decoy airfields, fake airfields to confuse enemy planes. They could be lit up at night to look like runways, and one was bombed by night bombers 174 times. One was built at Stawell to protect the Royal Ordnance Factory at Puriton and Bridgwater's factories as well as Westonzoyland aerodrome.

A German Heinkel bomber shot down over Puriton. It was said that the pilot had been to Bristol and did not want to bomb a city he knew and loved.

Opposite: *People got to know how to recognise German planes from British. Sometimes German aircrew machine gunned the people in the streets. You would need to know whether to take cover. The Observer Corps watched for German planes. They telephoned central control to send off fighter planes to attack enemy bombers.*

A "Sunday Dispatch" Page To Help Everyone Defend The Country

THE War Office has issued these diagram pictures of enemy troop-carrying 'planes. They are intended to guide Local Defence Volunteers and all members of the public.

Some of these pictures have been published elsewhere in the past few days, but this page contains many more details and also silhouettes of comparable British bombers. It is the only complete chart. Cut it out and hang it on your wall.

If you see an aeroplane that resembles an enemy, tell the police, an air raid warden, or the L.D.V. at once.

Here are some simple points to remember :
If the 'plane has more than two engines it is *probably* a German.

The 3-engined Junkers Ju 52 has one engine in the nose, looking like the head of a fly. These have been the 'planes most used for parachutists.

The Junkers Ju 90 has wings that sweep backwards like a swallow in flight.

Note the square-cut edges of the wings and tails of the Junkers 'planes.

If a bomber is flying low in daylight, note the colour.
British bombers are mostly painted black on the underside. (There are some silver or light green.)

The badge painted on British 'planes is like a red, white, and blue target, with the red as the bull's-eye.

German bombers are painted light blue-grey under the fuselage and wings.

Their badge is a black cross, outlined with a white band. The white band itself is outlined in black.

A black swastika is usually carried on the tail of the 'plane.

THESE ARE THE TYPES OF GERMAN AIRCRAFT YOU ARE MOST LIKELY TO SEE

Junkers JU 52
The Junkers 52 is the most important troop carrier and the one normally used by the Germans for parachute troops. It has a wing span of 96 feet and a length of 62 feet. Its distinctive features are :
1. Three engines.
2. Low wing.
3. Single square-cut rudder.
4. Sharply tapered wings.
5. Square-cut wing tips and tail plane.
6. Fixed undercarriage.

Junkers JU 86
Distinctive features of the Junkers 86, which has a wing span of 73ft. 5in. and a length of 57ft. 4in., are :
1. Two engines.
2. Low wing.
3. Two square-cut rudders.
4. Sharply tapered wings.
5. Square-cut wing tips and tail plane.
6. Retractable undercarriage.

Junkers JU 90
The Junkers 90, the biggest of the Junkers bombers, has a wing span of 115ft. and is 86ft. long. Its distinctive features are :
1. Four engines.
2. Low wing.
3. Two rudders.
4. Tapered wings.
5. Leading edge of wing has very pronounced sweep back.
6. Square-cut wing tips and tail plane.
7. Retractable undercarriage.

Focke-Wulf 200
The Focke-Wulf 200 Condor has a wing span of 108 feet and is 78 feet long. Its principal features are :
1. Four engines.
2. Low wing.
3. Single rudder.
4. Tapered wings.
5. Rounded wing tips and tail plane.
6. Retractable undercarriage.
7. Smooth stream-lined fuselage.

BUT DON'T MISTAKE THEM FOR THESE BRITISH BOMBERS

Whitley IV
Twin-engined long-range bomber. Undercarriage retracts. Rectangular fuselage, slightly tapered wings. Twin fins and rudders. Wing span, 84ft. 9in. ; length, 69ft. 3in.

Hampden
Twin-engined Handley Page Hampden long-range bomber. Undercarriage retracts. Deep, narrow, rectangular fuselage with rounded transparent nose. Twin fins and rudders. Highly tapered wings. Wing span 69ft. 2in. ; length, 53ft. 7in.

Lockheed Hudson B-14
Twin-engined bomber. Undercarriage retracts. Deep, short fuselage with twin fins and rudders and cantilever tailplane. Highly tapered wings with pointed tips. Wing span, 65ft. 6in. ; length, 44ft. 2¼in.

Cut Out This "Sunday Dispatch" Page And Pin It On The Wall At Home Or At Your Office

Blenheim
Twin-engined Bristol Blenheim Mk. I long-range fighter and high-speed bomber. Retracting undercarriage. Fixed tail wheel. Short transparent nose, straight tapered wings with pointed tips, deep motor nacelles, blanked by wings. Single fin and rudder. Wing span 56ft. 4in. ; length 39ft. 9in.

Wellington
Twin-engined Wellington Mk. Ia long-range bomber. Power-operated turret in nose with two guns. Similar turret in tail. Undercarriage retracts backwards. Deep, well-streamlined fuselage. Highly tapered wings. Tall single fin and rudder and cantilever tailplane. Wing span 86ft. 1in. ; length, 61ft. 3in.

HOW TO SPOT PARATROOPS

BADGE OF PARACHUTIST AFTER SIX DESCENTS

HELMET WITH WINGED BADGE
TWO CHIN STRAPS
ROLLED CAPE
BINOCULARS
PISTOL
HAVERSACKS
BOMB POCKETS
WATERBOTTLE

WILL HITLER INVADE US?

On 16 July 1940 Hitler announced that he would invade Britain. He hoped that Britain would surrender. German planes dropped leaflets telling Britain not to fight. Their bombers started attacking on 8 August *Adlertag* (Eagle Day). On 29 August they dropped high explosive bombs on Galmington, Bishop's Hull and Norton Fitzwarren.

THE BATTLE OF BRITAIN

Hitler had to destroy the RAF to win the battle – he couldn't invade by sea because Britain had more ships. The Luftwaffe had more planes than the RAF and 10,000 pilots; the RAF only had 1500 pilots. The British could build 400 Spitfires and Hurricanes per month so the Germans tried to bomb Bristol's and Yeovil's plane factories.

Rachel Reckitt described a 'dog-fight':
We had a marvellous view of an air fight so high up, that nothing but the extraordinary patterns of the frozen exhausts (vapour trails) could be seen. ...Sometimes the German planes, which could be distinguished by their close formation, which left three exhaust tracks tight together, were flying exactly into the tail of their own track. It all seems like slow motion – you see our fighters coming in at an angle to attack, but so slowly, apparently, that you can tell before if they will be in time or not. The fight lasted nearly an hour.

Four Heinkel bombers were the first enemy aircraft shot down in Somerset over Puriton in August, 1940. Part of one is in the Museum in Taunton. Crashed planes were kept on the site which is now Tesco's in Taunton. A German Dornier plane was exhibited in Vivary Park. You had to pay 6d. (2½p) which went to the Red Cross.

On 12 October 1940 Hitler gave up the idea of invading Britain – on 22 June 1941, he invaded Russia. Church bells were going to be the warning for an invasion, so through most of the war, church bells were kept silent.

6
Bombing

Docks like Cardiff suffered heavy attacks. Factories and electricity stations were another target. A total of 60,000 bombs fell on Somerset. 668 people were killed by bombs here, 665 seriously injured, 943 others injured, and 35,000 buildings were damaged or destroyed. High explosive bombs blew up a building. Planes also dropped incendiaries which did not burst into flame until a while after landing. In Exeter fire was 'the deadliest enemy. Some fires happened in locked premises so fire services could not get in'. People were taught how to pick them up with a garden fork and put them in sand or water. You could see 'little boys in Bristol running about with dustbin lids "bagging incendiaries"'. Also in Bristol one twelve-year-old girl modestly announced on arrival at a New Year's

Lieutenant Andrews was awarded the George Cross for his bravery in tackling a bomb alone – he made his men take shelter while he dealt with it. He and his men defused bombs that might explode. He saved Guy's Hospital from an unexploded bomb.

Eve party that she had put out nine fire bombs on the way.

In big fires you needed a lot of hoses. There wasn't always enough water to fight fires so water tanks were made in the towns. Children floated toy boats on them. The one in Yeovil ended up with fish in it. Men – and women – did fire-watching at night to see that buildings didn't catch fire.

Unexploded bombs got stuck and could blow up at any time. The Royal Engineers dug up unexploded bombs and defused them. This was very brave as they could – and did – blow up any time. Bombs sank deep into the soft earth in fields.

People used to go out to watch the planes.
The planes flew over Brompton Ralph every night at about six p.m. on their way to Wales, mainly Cardiff. Searchlights sweeping round were quite blinding. Sometimes machine-gun bullets whistled past the window. Some people used to walk up to Raleigh's Cross to watch across the Channel – it was like a fireworks display.

(Somerset Within Living Memory. Somerset Federation of Women's Institutes)

But as planes returned home they dropped their left-over bombs:

3 Jan 1941 Raid last night was over Cardiff and the loud crump we heard about 11.30 was a bomb on the recreation ground at Bishop's Lydeard. It has made a lovely excavation for a swimming pool.

(Anne Lee Michell's diary).

Eric Saffin heard it too. *One bomb landed in a field near Bishop's Lydeard Station and made a terrific hole of I'd say 50 feet across and 25 feet deep. It came down in the late evening and my father who had heard shells whistling in the first war actually heard this one, as he was shaving, and with soap all over his face he warned us to get down. It landed a mile away but it made everything jump and rattle.*

As the war went on, fewer bombs fell over Britain. The Germans developed rockets in 1944 but they couldn't reach as far as the South West.

THE BLACKOUT

Night was dangerous, that was when enemy bombers flew overhead. Children were indoors in the dark. Towns and cities have bright lights everywhere which would make it very easy for planes to see where to drop bombs, so the Government plan was to make everybody 'black out' their windows at night with dark curtains. ARP wardens went round to check. 'Put that light out' was a familiar order.

Keeping the towns and traffic blacked out helped to save them from being seen by enemy bombers, but there were lots of accidents in the dark. Cyclists and pedestrians couldn't always see cars coming as their headlights had covers that only allowed a slit of light.

It was gloomy in the dark streets. John Freeth was a soldier on his way to Egypt via South Africa. In Durban:

We were amazed to see the city a blaze of lights. It takes our breath away to see so many lights again in town, after groping in black-out darkness for three years.

After the war when lighting used far more electricity, they had to build extra electricity works, like Portishead B.

SOMERSET TOWNS – AND NEIGHBOURS

Every village or area had a warden in the ARP (Air Raid Precautions) who wore a uniform and a helmet with W on it. They looked after people in an air raid. They made sure lights didn't show so that planes couldn't see where to attack. When enemy aircraft were coming, they sounded the siren for 'alert' to go into shelters (and 'all clear' when they were gone). They checked on buckets of water and sand to put out fires. Some ARP were trained to rescue people out of bombed buildings and give first aid. They had to learn about gases, ropes, propping up broken walls, how to use acetylene cutters. R.N. Willey was awarded the George medal for rescuing people trapped under a table in a collapsed building at the Circus Tavern, Bath.

Bristol was badly bombed and the centre was flattened. A woman remembers how you could see the bright light of Bristol burning miles away at Congresbury where she lived.

The natural history gallery of Bristol Museum. Many precious things were destroyed when the museum was bombed.

Bristol, Yeovil and Weston-super-Mare's aircraft factories were attacked night after night. Yeovil suffered ten raids. On 11 April, 1941 – Good Friday – there was a raid with several delayed action bombs. A boy in bed had the wardrobe – open – fall on his bed which protected him from injury. There were five dead, 14 injured, 7 buildings destroyed and 182 damaged. Weston-super-Mare was targeted because of its aircraft factory. There was a raid on the 28 and 29 June, 1942 where people were

*…in the open putting out fires and rescuing those who were trapped. Often they had to run for shelter as bombs whistled down and machine gun bullets splattered about them. Some of the raiding aircraft dived so low they had to take avoiding action to clear high build-*ings, and one actually flew along a wide street level with the first floor windows. The town was lit up as brightly as noon.*

Hitler made raids on the beautiful cathedral cities like Bath and Exeter.

Bath
Planes roared down to 50 feet, and shot at people on streets and buildings with cannon and machine gun fire. The houses round the station were more damaged than the grand part of the town. Rachel Reckitt went to help people find somewhere to live. She described the

clatter of broken glass, and every few minutes time bombs going off, and soldiers dashing about, hoses all over the roads and everything covered with thick white dust.

Exeter
Philip Binding was a little boy staying with grandparents in Taunton:
We could see the orange sky to the South when Exeter was the target of a raid which reduced the whole of the city centre to a smoking ruin with the exception of the Cathedral. It was a frightening thought that there were Germans up there in the sky who could do such terrible things to human beings and small children like myself who would never live long enough perhaps to know what on earth all the argument was about.

Illustrated London News

Bath (and many other ancient cities like Exeter) were damaged by bombs and many people were killed.

It took a long time until houses could be mended: 'rows and rows of houses with windows blasted out, trying to make the best of a bad job with boards and old curtains.' Somewhere to live had to be provided for those made homeless. Many had nowhere to go. Bombing was terrifying for every-one, especially small children.

Some families had a shelter in the garden and others had a Morrison shelter, like a table, indoors. Philip Binding said:

I well remember the Morrison shelter put in what was the dining room. If the siren went (and what a ghastly heart-stopping banshee wail it set up, being mounted on a telegraph pole almost opposite the house) we would be awakened and pound down the stairs and fling ourselves panting into this steel-girdered framed shelter, covered in heavy-duty mesh wire which occupied pride of place in the room. It was all very exciting because you saw for the only time in your life parents and grandpar-ents in their night attire, making out that it was a jolly occasion when in fact you could see that they were pretty terrified. There were occasions when the heavy ack-ack guns at the end of Stoke Road opened up and I can well recall searchlights probing the night sky being visible if you took a peek out of the window.

Invasion of Britain

1.7.40	Channel Islands occupied by the Germans
8.8.40	*Adlertag* (Eagle Day) German attack on Britain begins **Blitz**
	42,000 killed, 50,000 injured in blitz in British cities 1940-4
15.9.40	185 German planes shot down over London
31.9.40	The Battle of Britain ends
12.10.40	Hitler abandons invasion of Britain
15.11.42	Church bells ring for first time to celebrate victory in North Africa
20.4.43	Church bells can be rung again, fears of invasion over but still hold invasion exercise.

Somerset Bombing from 1940

18 June	Flax Bourton
19 and 20 June	Thornfalcon and West Hatch
25 June	Bristol
1 July	Bath bridge, road and GWR out of action
	From then till mid Dec. every night and day attacks
	High explosives fell on remote places
29 Aug.	Fell on Galmington, Bishops Hull and Norton Fitzwarren
Sept.	S. Wales
25 Sept.	Filton Bristol Aeroplane Company bombed – 72 killed, 166 injured (19 died later) in shelters
27 Sept.	Plane brought down on Portbury Beach
1941	24 Nov. onwards Bristol raids
25.4.42	Bath – evacuees there, also Navy

The Battle of the Atlantic

7

'With enough U-boats we can and will finish off the British Isles', said Admiral Donitz. He planned to starve the British so that we would give in to Hitler. Ships were attacked from the first month of the war:

HMS Courageous *(aircraft carrier) sunk on Sunday 5 Taunton men lost.*

(*Gazette* 23.9.39)

Fishermen's boat bombed and men machine-gunned.

(*Gazette* 30.12.39)

The Hydrographic Office, who moved to Taunton in 1939, produced charts for ships. They marked all the wrecks and mines. In shallow water the wrecks stuck out and other ships could be damaged by them.

HMS Vortigern, *which was hit by two torpedoes and sunk in an engagement in the North Sea on Saturday night, was the adopted ship of the Isle of Dogs School at Wells. Each month the teachers and children brought gifts that were dispatched to the crew, and only recently we published several appreciative letters from the*

Commanding Officer and members of the crew thanking the school for parcels of comforts so regularly sent.

(*Wells Journal* 20.3.42)

Even before they joined in the war, American ships were sometimes sunk by German submarines. Japanese planes attacked the American fleet in Pearl Harbor on 7 December, 1941 and the USA then declared war on Japan and Germany. Now Britain and the USA could take on the U boats together, building longer range planes, the 'Catalina' and 'Liberator', helped by long range radar to detect submarines in the sea and depth charges to destroy them. Liberators were stationed at Dunkeswell and Upottery airfields. President Kennedy's brother Joseph was based here. They made raids on the ports in France where the German submarines were being built. He was killed in a plane carrying explosives. In 1943 the Allies began to clear the seas of U boats.

Hans Gobeler (from Germany) said:
When I was seventeen, I joined the navy. I was proud to

be a submarine man. I recognised what danger it was to be on a submarine. … We saw that each time when we came back, there was a big hole in more boats. We couldn't count them. We knew we lost the battle of the Atlantic. From 39,000 submarine men, 32,000 were killed at sea. Most of them very young men.

Shipping

23.9.39	HMS *Courageous* (aircraft carrier) sunk on Sunday, 5 Taunton men lost
30.12.39	Fishermen's boat bombed and men machine-gunned
By end of 1940	728,000 tons of food and animal foodstuffs had been sunk
Sept.-Dec. 1940	Loss of food in air attacks = 159,000 tons damaged
16-20 March 1943	German submarines sink 21 British ships in Atlantic

8

Scrimping and Saving, Making Do and Mending

Britain had always imported food and materials. Now the U-boats and mines cut off supplies, people had to manage with what was produced here, coal for trains rather than petrol for cars. There weren't enough metals, wood, paper, oil... Japan controlled rubber from Malaya.

Salvage meant Recycling :
    bones for explosives
    metals for armaments
    rubber for re-using
    paper and rags for shell cases
    kitchen waste – for pigs '6000 tons feeds 5-6000 pigs'

METAL

All spare metal in towns was sent for scrap; railings were cut off, even from graves. (You can sometimes still see the stumps in low walls.) Wells and Taunton sent old Russian cannon (from the Crimean War) and a First World War tank from Vivary Park.

A First World War tank in French Weir, Taunton. Various historical items were sent to be melted down, like cannon brought back from the Crimean War.

SERVICE | COMMERCIALS SUPPLIED.

STROUD HOUSE

BRITISH RED CROSS SOCIETY

SCRAP METAL DUMPED HERE WILL HELP US AND

YOUR BIT HELPS

BRITISH RED CROSS SOCIETY

DO IT NOW

IRON · BRASS · LEAD DIG OUT THAT JUNK

FIRST WEEK £1-10-0

METAL FOR MUNITIONS DUMP   IN AID OF RED CROSS BRING YOURS NOW

Saucepans collected at Wells. Aluminium was needed for making aircraft. Appeals for saucepans brought huge piles.

PAPER

Paper was very short. Newspapers were rationed to a few pages. You had to take your own paper with you to wrap your groceries. Books were collected for the troops to read. Langport Book Drive raised 27,000 books. Three were given to the British Museum 'to replace others destroyed in air raids'.

Opposite: *The government encouraged everybody to play their part. 'Metals for munitions' was the slogan at this collecting point.*

COAL

Coal was needed for steam trains and for electricity stations. Factories needed electricity to keep going so ordinary people were told to save fuel. In the Mendip mines the miners were mostly older men and there weren't enough of them. Ernest Bevin, Minister for Supplies (who came from Somerset), sent young men to the mines instead of into the Forces. They were called the 'Bevin Boys'.

Shortages

4.7.41	Coal rationing begins
11.7.40	Aluminium pots and pans requested for melting for aircraft
15.12.41	Government increases appeal for scrap metal
18.12.41	People urged to take fewer baths in less water and share bath water

Clothes Rationing

2.6.41	Rationing introduced for clothes
3.12.42	Utility clothing introduced to save cloth
15.3.42	Embroidery banned on women's underwear
13.1.43	School uniforms must be grey or blue to save on dye
1.2.44	Clothes rationing ends

CLOTHING

Mothers re-made clothes. A grown-up's coat could be cut down to fit a child. One magazine suggested cutting off the top of socks to sew onto the arms of a jumper if it was too small!

Towns competed to collect money to build a Spitfire or ship. This money box was made to encourage the boy who owned it to save for a ship.

Parachutes made of silk or nylon were made into nighties and underwear and even wedding dresses. Meg Paul made her wedding dress out of net curtains!

If you were getting married, or if you had lost everything when your house was bombed, you were given extra clothing rations. Most of the factories that had made clothes were now making uniforms and there were very few making household goods. The government had a 'utility mark' scheme which showed that things were good quality.

As well as saving everything at home, there were campaigns to get towns to buy a Spitfire or contribute to a destroyer. Towns competed to give the most in 'Wings for Victory' Week. Buckland St Mary held a dance, skittles, and a whist drive in aid of the warship fund.

9
Travel

Trains were the main way of travelling – they were steam trains running on British coal. All the evacuees went by train. They were crowded out with troops and evacuees and people fleeing bombing. All supplies were moved by train. When Exeter was bombed the railway lines were damaged. Weston had road bridges over the railway damaged.

Car owners were given a ration of petrol until spring, 1943, when it stopped altogether. They had to leave their cars in a garage untill the end of the war. There was very little traffic and in villages children could play in the road. The only cars were army vehicles. Road signs were removed. When the American forces came to Britain they got lost so in 1943 the signs were put back.

Cars had to have covers over their lights so that planes could not see them from above. Nothing else could either. *Somerset road deaths. Majority in black out. 42 killed, 25 in blackout in last 4 months of 1939,* said the *Gazette* 17.2.40.

Posters pushed home the message that the railways were needed to move troops about. As there was next to no petrol, everything and everybody had to go by rail. Trains were so crowded that many people had to stand for long journeys.

Signpost with no signs. They were taken down so that if the enemy invaded, they wouldn't know where they were. They were put back to help the American forces when they came to Britain.

Opposite: *Bus with gas trailer. Some buses and lorries tried experiments with other fuels. It helped but they were very big and awkward.*

Cycling was a useful way of getting about during the war. Farms had horses and carts and some started to use them again when they had no petrol, but sometimes there were accidents like:

Horse bolts and cart overturns – Hemyock death.

(*Gazette 31.10.42*)

A farmer died when an American truck collided with his horse and cart at Westonzoyland.

If you wanted to go to the cinema or a dance, you had to walk, so village halls put on a lot more entertainment. It was more fun for the young with all the extra people about, especially American servicemen who looked so smart and 'talked like film-stars'.

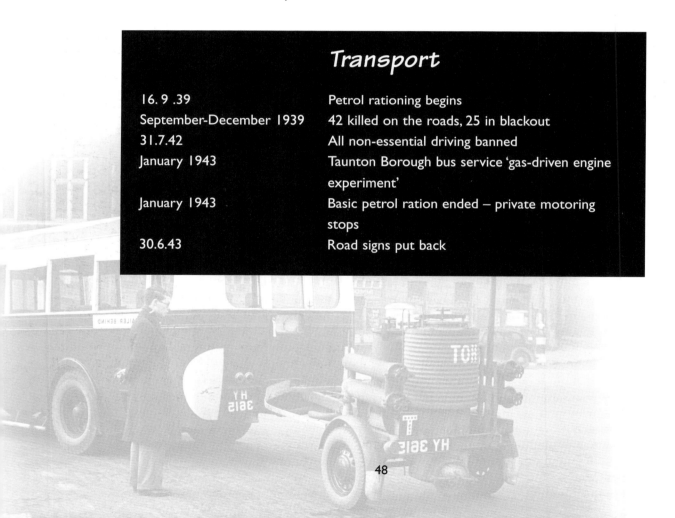

Transport

16.9.39	Petrol rationing begins
September–December 1939	42 killed on the roads, 25 in blackout
31.7.42	All non-essential driving banned
January 1943	Taunton Borough bus service 'gas-driven engine experiment'
January 1943	Basic petrol ration ended – private motoring stops
30.6.43	Road signs put back

Barrage balloons floated above some towns to keep off bombers; aircraft would want to keep away from the wires that hung between them.

Hitler and Goering and Goebbels as the horsemen or 'dark riders' of the apocalypse, bringing death, famine, plague and destruction.

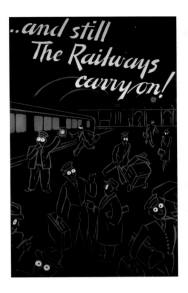

Government posters encouraged everybody to work together for victory or 'do their bit'.

'The Old Privy' (or outside loo), by Syd Durston. The country areas of Somerset did not have main drains so the smelly loo was at the bottom of the garden. Newspaper was cut into squares for toilet paper. At night you needed a candle.

'Trying to make an early start' by Syd Durston. Peat diggers are trying to start the engine by cranking the starting handle. The chickens roam freely instead of being cooped up in battery cages.

Syd Durston paints scenes of his boyhood in the country during the war. The boys have leant how to catch rabbits, a luxury when meat was rationed. Here a rabbit is being pulled out of a pipe beneath a gateway but it has found a bolt hole and escaped.

'Breaking the Ice' by Syd Durston. During the war hay was still made with all its seed intact and put in a rick. When it was frosty in the winter the hay was cut and carried out to the cattle. The seed that dropped kept the small birds alive, especially in cold winters like 1940-41. The ice had to be broken for the cattle to drink.

'Trevor Jones reading the News' by Syd Durston. Trevor was the only boy in Catcott School to have a radio. Trevor would write his own version of the news, sit on the wall under an old oak tree and read it to his classmates.

'Killing rats' by Syd Durston. The men have finished threshing the corn mow [rick] and they move the staddle to kill the rats which have been living on the corn. Men and dogs kill the rats – sometimes over a hundred – to save the precious food supplies.

'Washing Day' by Syd Durston. Women's work was hard in the country without washing machines and electricity.

10
Food

29 September, 1939 was National Registration Day. Each householder had to fill in a form to say how many people lived in their household for identity cards and ration books. 8 January 1940 was 'Coupon Monday' when food rationing began for butter, cheese, bacon and sugar. The amounts went up and down; the cheese ration was 2 ozs. (50 grs.) at one time but when it went down to 1 oz., it was difficult for grocers to cut such small pieces. Farm workers and vegetarians had extra cheese. Meat rationing began on 11 March 1940. People were very fed up when tea was rationed. There wasn't any coffee, only 'Camp Coffee' made of burnt sugar.

One little boy noticed how grumpy the family got when one person wasn't fair:

The meagre food allowances ...were incredibly little by today's standards and Percy, having a hearty appetite, tended to wolf a whole week's allowance at one sitting. This was the cause of some remonstration or even altercations which broke out from time to time as he so wantonly broke the limits of self-discipline. (Philip Binding)

Scientific advisers helped the Government plan food rationing to have a fair share for all, relying as much as possible on what Britain could produce. People

Icing sugar was banned on cakes so wedding cakes had cardboard icing instead.

were urged to eat potatoes (home grown) rather than bread as wheat had to be imported. There was one standard bread, the 'National Wheatmeal'. Sugar was scarce. *I can vividly remember longing for sweets. We all gave up sugar in drinks so that it could be used in cake making.*

Sometimes people went to restaurants and cafés; you didn't have to take your precious coupons unless it was expensive (over 5 shillings (25p)).

'British Restaurants' provided cheap meals... *we used to go most afternoons when school was out. Occasionally we would go by bus to Yeovil and have tea at the British Restaurant housed in the Liberal Hall, or have tea at the Cottage Café – bread and butter, jam, a cake and tea, four shillings and sixpence for the four of us, all helping stretch household rations. How we appreciated those treats.*

(Somerset Within Living Memory. Somerset Federation of Women's Institutes.)

Children didn't know about oranges or bananas or fruit from abroad (though it must have been hard for grown-ups who didn't have them anymore). I can remember being given an orange by American soldiers and not knowing what to do with it.

Woman sent a banana by relative in Gibraltar – offered it as prize in charity event – it raised £1.16.6d (£1 .83p – more than a week's wages).

(Gazette 17.7.43)

The Fruit Research Station at Long Ashton, near Bristol, developed Ribena, from British-grown black-currants. Rose hips were collected by the WVS and other volunteers to give children vitamin C in rose hip syrup.

Dig for Victory

The government wanted to grow more food in Britain. If you had a garden, you could grow fruit and vegetables and even keep chickens and bees. Parks and playing fields were dug up to make allotments so that people could grow a lot of extra food. Britain grew 1,000,000 tons on allotments. They were friendly places. Philip Binding: *We had an allotment and I recall learning*

> *'In 1944*
> *Hitler went to war.*
> *He lost his pants*
> *in the middle of France*
> *and never went there no more.'*

Not everybody knew about gardening so an allotment was made in the park to show people what to do: *Demonstration allotment in Vivary Park produced crops to weight of 18 cwts., 22 lbs.. (924 kilos) and worth £22.13.4d (£22.67p).*

(*Gazette* 20.6.42)

After the German army occupied France and then Jersey, onions and tomatoes couldn't be brought to Britain. With an allotment you could grow your own. Some people tried growing tobacco, but it was difficult to dry it to make into cigarettes. Fertilisers were short. Some hairdressers used hair in the bottom of a trench in the garden to grow runner beans (hair produces nitrogen).

'Veg for Victory'; the V sign stood for Victory and was marked on everything. Some parks had areas given over to allotments. Bridgwater Parks Department made this display of what they produced.

My father owned our house at Milborne Port, set in four acres of land. We had four goats and mother produced cheese and butter from the milk, a Wessex Saddleback pig named Henry and an accredited poultry breeding station. This meant we got a special ration of fowl food and sent (by rail) hatching eggs and day old chicks all over the country. The garden had many fruit trees and a large amount of vegetables. We had four hives of bees and with chickens etc. we were almost self supporting during the war.

(Somerset Within Living Memory. Somerset Federation of Women's Institutes.)

Keeping food was difficult as houses didn't have fridges. (The government had big refrigerated food storage depots. Huge amounts were stored at Norton Fitzwarren for the troops.) If you had a good crop of fruit you could have extra sugar to make jam and the WI gave lessons in how to keep fruit in cans. The egg ration was only one per week so keeping chickens was popular.

Food Rationing

29.9.39	National Registration Day – everyone registers for identification cards and ration books
9.10.39	Act of Parliament stops people charging too much for food
8.1.40	'Coupon Monday' food rationing begins for butter, bacon, sugar and meat
11.3.40	Meat rationing begins
27.7.42	Sweet rationing
25.10.42	Milk ration reduced to 2 ½ pints per week
25.10.42	Icing sugar banned on cakes
22.2.44	Lemons available again for Shrove Tuesday pancakes

12 Farming

Many British farms were poor and didn't have up-to-date equipment. When the threat of war came close, the government put money into farms to help them modernise and produce more. The Ministry of Food told them what they were going to produce so they couldn't choose.

Very few farms had electricity or much machinery. Without machinery, the work needed a lot of workers, but in 1940 10,000 agricultural workers were called up. How could farms have enough farm workers? The answer was the Women's Land Army and Prisoners of War.

WOMEN'S LAND ARMY

Women volunteered to join the WLA (Women's Land Army). Some came from farming families but they came from cities too. They were given some training by the agricultural college at Cannington or Steanbow Farm, Pilton, and they were often good with new machinery, like a milking machine.

The advertisers announced that the machine was so simple that a landgirl could operate it. Well, the young generation was the machine minded one, even on the distaff [women's] side; besides, a girl would not have to be paid as much as a married man.
(Monica M. Hutchings *The Chronicles of Church Farm*)

Women didn't earn as much as men. Landgirls earned 28/- (£1.40p) if over eighteen, 22/6 (£1.12 ½p) under

Land girls with a lorry in Congresbury with their slogan This happy breed we help to feed. *They were taking part in a celebration at the end of the war.*

Land girl ploughing with a tractor. Tractors were needed when there was a shortage of men to work on the farms but with the shortage of petrol, horses were more useful.

Land girls with piglets and chicks. A happy picture of farm life which doesn't show the cold and the wet!

eighteen. They mostly stayed in hostels or on the farm. They were provided with dungarees, mack, shirts, breeches, green pullover, shoes and boots, and, later, a hat. The first woman to register with the Land Army was Valerie Hodge, an artist from Bristol who joined in spring, 1939. She joined because it helped rather than destroyed life.

PRISONERS OF WAR...

also were used for farm work. Some farmers said the Italians didn't work hard enough – they preferred playing football – but another said the Italian who worked for him was the son of a farmer and was marvellous. I can remember them waving when they were working in the fields. They liked children and missed their families. The Germans were good, reliable workers. Some preferred to stay in Britain at the end of the war.

CATTLE

Somerset grass is fresh and green with all the rain so cows produce good milk. The Ministry of Food decided that Somerset should continue to produce milk; they kept registers of all the milk and who made butter and cheese and how much. It was difficult for farmers to make cheese for their own families. They weren't allowed to make cream as it was a luxury. I can remember having whipped cream on bread and jam when I was about six staying on a farm – I had never tasted it before. As there were few milking machines and milking by hand was slow, herds were usually not more than thirty cattle. It could take half the morning to milk that many. Sometimes a boy would be employed to help with the milking. I can remember Jack squirting me with milk from the cow's udder. It was a hard job looking after cows; you had to be up at four or five o'clock to milk them. It was difficult to take a day off – you had to find someone else to milk them instead. Milk cost less in the West than in the cities. The government wanted food to be cheap.

TB (tuberculosis) was a problem; there were only four 'attested' herds in Somerset (tested to prove they were free from TB). Foot and Mouth disease affected cattle in the war – 10,000 animals were slaughtered in 1942. People wondered whether foot and mouth germs had been dropped in enemy bombs because the Germans had dropped Colorado beetles on potato crops on Isle of Wight (children went to spot them and collect them).

PLOUGHING UP THE GRASSLANDS

Farmers were fined if they left any land wild. Areas where there was bracken were ploughed to give more potatoes or wheat. After the war these areas went on being ploughed which must have been a loss to wild life.

A Land Army girl remembers working on Elworthy Barrows in the Brendon hills:
It was cold and pouring with rain, and there was a dense fog. I met a gang of other Land Army girls. With each gang there was a forewoman and a foreman to tell us what to do. We were given staff hooks and told to cut the heather and gorse bushes off at ground level. This was very tough work. When we had finished, we went back to the beginning and planted the moor with potatoes. When we harvested them we were amazed at the wonderful crop. It made it all seem worthwhile.

From 1942 Fordson tractors began to be imported from the USA. It was often the Land Girls who had the skills to deal with them; they had been trained and were young and adaptable.

HORSES
Horses were still used on farms. When you couldn't get petrol, a horse and cart could take you shopping as well as working on the farm. The only problem was when they needed shoeing as many blacksmiths had been called up. Cart horses were very patient and reliable.
The strength, patience and willingness of these huge
horses was something to wonder at, said Eric Saffin.

In North Petherton the milk round used pony and trap, with milk churn. Two Land girls asked to take the pony out for an afternoon but it would only go on its usual round with stops at every house!

Meg Paul trained as a tractor driver. At the end of the course she was asked if she would like to be one of the instructors.
You had to understand the engine and how it worked. Tractors had various ploughs etc. to be added on. I used to sing on the tractor. I loved it.

She looked after sheep with an old shepherd. In the very cold winter, 1946/7, a lot of lambs died — lambing was in January. Sheep were not brought in, they made a shelter for them with straw bales.

DAYLIGHT
Double Summer Time — the clocks went on two hours in summer and stayed one hour ahead in winter — this meant that it was light in summer until midnight. Farmer's wives worked all the hours God gave — and now extra ones too! In the dark of winter blackout rules made it difficult to see to the animals. Milking began at 4 am. In summer they could be still working at 10 pm.

FLAX

Somerset produced good flax to make linen. There was a flax factory at Lopen and at Crewkerne making webbing for soldiers' kit and harness for parachutes.

CHICKENS...

Chickens weren't kept in big sheds as they are today, farmers let them roam in the fields. *Gleaning ...to save the time spent gathering the ears of corn missed by the harvester, the hen house would be moved out into the cornfield and the hens would glean for themselves.* (Eric Saffin)

...AND RABBITS

People didn't hunt foxes during the war and sometimes a fox might kill a chicken, but mostly foxes caught rabbits. There were millions of rabbits then; you could see a field full of them.

Country children were used to animals being killed; it came as a shock to town children. Philip Binding remembered

...rabbit stew and the use of rabbit skins when sewn together as loose mats or covers. I was fascinated and horrified at the sight of rabbits being skinned and revealed in all their bloody nakedness with those bulging senseless eyes after the last of their vesture was peeled off.

Farming

11.3.39	Milk scheme for children Government tells farmers not to make cream; need permit to make butter
1.7.39	Women's Land Army (WLA) formed
23.12.39	1,500, 000 acres brought under the plough
1942	Nearly 10,000 animals slaughtered because of foot and mouth
1945	276,641 horses on farms (cf. 1939 16,758 horses working on farms)
1945	13, 565 regular workers on Somerset farms, 1223 land girls, 841 POWs.

13 Prisoners of War in Somerset

All through the war soldiers could be taken prisoner if their side was losing or if they got stranded in the wrong place. Somerset had about ten Prisoner of War (POW) camps. You can see the statue of Romulus and Remus made by an Italian Prisoner of War where Stoberry Park Camp was, near Wells. Goathurst Camp's stone entrance is still there. They had about 15 timber or concrete huts, each with two cast iron stoves. They were surrounded by a barbed wire fence.

Goathurst held 700 Italian POWs. They were allowed to live and work on farms, and to visit the cinema at Bridgwater. They wore dark brown uniforms with yellow circular and diamond patches. The prisoners made rings and toys they carved out of wood. One Italian was a tailor so on wet days when he couldn't do farm work he made clothes for the children. As one boy was playing in fairly deep water with his friends on a raft they made, he got caught underneath it. An Italian POW saved his life. John Salvatore was captured in Tunisia. He was sent to Goathurst. He had to do hedging, ditching, whatever work was needed. He was paid 5d. per day, not in currency but camp tokens which they could exchange for cigarettes, etc. (They were given 1 packet of cigarettes every week.) John worked on some very isolated farms. He walked to church in Minehead, 5 miles away. He went home to Sardinia in 1945 but decided to come back to Somerset in 1947.

Crowcombe Camp. German prisoners were relieved to see that camps were clean and well organised.

Fritz Wolff was captured in 1944 fighting against the Allies invading France. He was brought to Goathurst. The camp was in a beautiful area and they could even catch a glimpse of the sea. The huts were quite clean and new and conditions were good. They got the same rations as a soldier, which was more than the local civilians. The camp even had its own bakery. He was relieved to see how good the camp was, as the Nazis had told them they would be badly treated if they were taken prisoner. There were probably about 1000 men in the camp, rising to 1500 at one time at the end of the war. He returned home to his parents after the war but now that part of Germany was in the Russian zone so he returned to Britain. He said:

How much better it is for Europeans all to talk to each other as they do now, even if it means some give and take, rather than fighting wars as I had to do in my youth.

British prisoners of war all commented on how the Red Cross parcels helped them to survive. There was not enough food in Germany or Italy.
Red Cross parcels for POWs cost £4 million this year, join the penny-a-day scheme towards the parcels.

(Gazette 19.9.42)

Charles Dickens of Broomfield was taken prisoner in North Africa in 1942 by the Germans. They were

Gunther Anton was eighteen years old when he was taken to Houndstone Camp, near Yeovil. He ran a factory making glass in Germany after the war and gave new windows to East Chinnock Church in gratitude.

given 4 ½ ozs. (125 grs.) of bread per day, a tin of bully beef between three, and 1 pint water. There wasn't enough water. Twenty to thirty men died every day because there were no toilets or water for washing. After a month they were shipped to Naples, then Lucca. They were still wearing the clothes they were captured in. The Red Cross came in and brought them new clothes and food parcels. They didn't know what they would have done without the medical supplies from the Red Cross.

After Mussolini lost power, they hoped they would be freed but the Germans took over the camp. Charles escaped with some others in August. They went up into the mountains and walked towards the British troops but it took them until October. He changed his uniform for rags and could pass unnoticed by the Italians and Germans.

A German prisoner of war at the threshing machine with the Knight family. They worked hard on the farms. Some stayed or returned to England when East Germany came under the Russians.

Mothers and Foster-mothers

14

11 May 1941 *How hard it is to be a mother, farmer, housewife, WVS canteen worker etc. etc. all in one.* This is what Mrs Anne Lee Michell wrote in her diary which she kept for most of the war. She and her husband lived in Wellington with their two small children. Mrs Michell kept chickens and goats and grew vegetables on her allotment. They had lodgers

Taunton, Massachusetts, gave Taunton a mobile kitchen. Members of the Women's Voluntary Service (in the picture) could take it to give meals to the people after bombing raids in towns like Plymouth and Exeter.

and an American officer came to stay with his horse. (She was given 3/- (15p) per day for the officer and 3/9 (19½p) for the horse.) Mrs Michell worked for the WVS, driving expectant mothers to a maternity home in the Quantocks (14 miles from Wellington); she also ran a baby clinic. She went to bombed cities like Plymouth and Exeter with the mobile kitchen to provide food and drink for the bombed-out families and she did the night shift in a canteen in Taunton. From 1942 Mrs Michell went to work in a Wellington factory, Bell Brothers, who made air filters for the Air Ministry. She was checking batches of glass ampoules for flaws.

20 May. *Very busy clinic, weighed 28 babies, all yelling at once, one piddled all over us and another was sick. Pathetic little family who were buried alive for two hours in London in the last bad blitz. Tea with Mrs Stevens...*

21 May – *heart ache – all the troubles sit on one. Helped make fowl run for our new chickens this evening. Our allotment is sprouting beans.*

Women played an enormous part in the 'war effort'. Not only did they take in evacuees, have soldiers billeted on them, look after their own families, queue endlessly for food, dig for victory, feed

Women from the ATS (Auxiliary Territorial Service). From December, 1941 women without children had to go into the Forces.

be in the fashion · cover your hair

It was fashionable to have long 'film star' hair styles which could get caught in factory machinery so women were urged to tie their hair up.

animals, volunteer for the Women's Voluntary Service, Red Cross, Women's Land Army, but also they were expected to work in the factories, join the Forces and still look attractive! Women did a lot of jobs they had never done before during the war years. They learnt to drive for the WVS or in the Forces. They found themselves taking charge.

Women who were by now taking over jobs where men had been called into the Forces, started another small revolution. They started for the first time to wear trousers, at first to work and then as a wartime fashion. (Eric Saffin)

Women in the Forces often had a career and had a good time, going to dances and travelling.

Jackie Moggridge flew Spitfires to the bases where they were needed.

Jackie Moggridge learnt to fly Spitfires. Even those who stayed at home were busy knitting and sewing for the 'war effort':

Lyng. 13 pairs socks, one helmet and one scarf made by the knitting circle for troops as part of the Somerset Comforts Fund. (Gazette 12.10.40)

The Sister Susie Service for Soldiers offered to sew buttons or stripes, or wash or mend socks for soldiers. Women also sewed camouflage nets before the D-Day Invasion. These big nets had artificial leaves sewn on so that you could disguise lorries and jeeps under them. Women were taken by bus to the Brendon Hills from Nynehead to cut pit props from the trees there. Other women were building an aerodrome. But it was *Difficult to shop as everything is closed when we return from work*. There were no supermarkets then or late shopping. Queueing for food at all the different shops took a long time.

Like Mrs Michell, many women worked in factories: Ena Hawkins of Bridgwater made equipment for depth charge detonators (against submarines). Ena worked for eleven hours, with two weeks in the daytime and two on nights.

Mrs Gay Rampling worked at the Bristol Aeroplane Company in Weston-super-Mare producing Avro Anson planes. Women worked the same as the men; *Whatever the men did, we did – from painting to inspection to packing parachutes*. 40% of the workers making aircraft were women.

Daisy Parfitt worked for Scophony in Wells. She didn't know what she was making. The workers only knew that they were making aircraft parts. They had Workers' Playtime (on the radio) to keep them entertained. The canteen provided a good lunch. The firm also ran a day nursery and Daisy's son attended this from 8.30am to 6 pm every day. Daisy was promoted to being an inspector.

Women at War

1.7.39	WLA (Women's Land Army) formed
2.7.39	WAAF (Women's Auxiliary Air Force) formed
17.3.41	Women are urged to volunteer for jobs in factories
2.12.41	Unmarried women aged twenty-thirty called up for military service
25.4.42	Princess Elizabeth, aged sixteen, registers for war service
6.12.44	Queen Elizabeth thanks the women of Britain for their war work

Americans

15

The USA did not join the war at first, although they helped the British. Taunton, Massachusetts, gave a kitchen van to help provide people with food after an air raid. After the Japanese attacked the American fleet at Pearl Harbor in December, 1941, the USA joined the British against the Japanese and Germans. American troops came to Britain to invade France and defeat the Germans. They had camps all over Somerset.

Early in 1942 the first American troops appeared in Taunton. The first ones I saw were riding in a lorry... the rear of the lorry was covered with a round canvas hood that made it resemble the look of the wagons that the pioneers used to cross America.

(Eric Saffin)

They certainly had plenty of money to flash around. They used to sit on the low wall outside our neighbours' in South Road and just inside the wall was a tall evergreen hedge. It was not long before I found that in the litter just inside the wall at the bottom of the hedge were to be found many coins which had slipped out of the fashionably-cut trouser pockets of the GIs who sat on the wall.

(Philip Binding)

Jennifer, entertaining the wounded American troops in Musgrove Hospital. She looks like Shirley Temple, a popular child film-star.

65

American troops were very generous to children. *We children quickly found that we could qualify for hand-outs of sweets, chewing gum and perhaps the odd toy if we were very lucky.*

The Americans built Musgrove Park Hospital to look after their troops, especially as they knew many would be wounded when they invaded France on D-Day to fight the Germans.

BLACK AMERICANS

British people were shocked at the attitudes of the American Army towards black soldiers. The Second World War was supposed to be a fight for justice for all people and against Hitler's racist policies but the black soldiers were unfairly treated. In many places, such as Frome, white and black soldiers were allowed into town on alternate nights. Eric Saffin as a boy, observed what went on:

I think it used to annoy them that here in England anyone could sit anywhere on a bus or go into a pub or restaurant and more than one talked of the problems there would be after the war when these men would have to conform to the rules of segregation once more. The black GIs were more ready to please as they were so pleased at being treated as equals by someone who was white.

Americans

5.7.41	Presentation of mobile kitchen from Taunton, Massachusetts, in Vivary Park
7.12.41	USA fleet bombed by the Japanese at Pearl Harbor
6.6.44	D-Day. Allies land in Normandy
17.8.42	American Flying Fortress bombers make first raid on Germany
1943	Joseph Kennedy, older brother of President Kennedy, killed in plane
June 1944	1,650,000 USA troops in Britain on eve of D-Day

16
D-Day

6 June 1944 was D-Day (Deliverance Day) when the Allied Forces landed in Normandy to free western Europe from German occupation. South Somerset became one vast dump of ammunition and stores to be taken to the coast.

Eric Saffin was friendly with the Americans near Cotford:

As the date of the invasion grew nearer so did the volume of men and material gathered and stored in and around Taunton... We used to see vehicles that had been modified to drive through water. We saw Dakotas towing gliders in large numbers overhead. We said our good-byes to the GIs with whom we had become especially friendly. It was a nervy time as they knew some of them might not be going home afterwards.

Residents in the Vale of Taunton Deane who were awake during the first hour of 6th June 1944 saw the massed squadrons rising from the brightly-lit aerodrome at Merryfield, Ilminster. It was a truly spectacular sight. The sky over Taunton was temporarily filled with twinkling

lights, for, in addition to the normal navigation lights of peace time, each aircraft carried recognition lamps on the leading edge of the wings. The shrewd observer hazarded a guess that this was 'D' Day at last.'

(Recollections of D-Day by a Taunton resident)

Lisieux, Taunton's twin town, was badly damaged during the Invasion of Normandy, as were many towns where the Germans fought to keep control of France.

American planes lined up to take off from Dunkeswell for D-Day.

The Hydrographic Office (part of the Admiralty making charts for ships) was asked to provide all the information for choosing beaches for 26 to 30 divisions (about 600,000 men) to land. They had to be steep enough to bring boats in close but not too steep for troops to run up. The tide had to be high enough to take the boats up the beach but low enough to see obstacles in the water.

Imagine a dark night and fog swirling round; you are going with two boats to do some secret surveys on the beaches under the enemy's noses. You have two boats in case one breaks down, but you lose each other in the fog. You try signalling with a torch – but will the Germans see you? Luckily they didn't and they all came home safe with the surveys done. They made their charts to show how and where all the troops would go. In June they put buoys to guide ships and the floating harbour. The Nazis were taken by surprise. But many men were killed in the fighting. The French towns were badly damaged with gunfire and bombing. But the French were free at last.

D-Day

6.6.44	D-Day landings – invasion of France by Allies
June-September 44	V1 rockets attack London and South East
September 44 to 1945	V2 rocket attacks
4-11.2.45	Churchill, Stalin and Roosevelt meet at Yalta to decide future of Europe
29.4.45	German army in Italy surrenders
30.4.45	Hitler dead
7.5.45	Total surrender
8 May	VE day

17
VE Day

Victory in Europe only came when Hitler was dead. He wouldn't surrender so the fighting went on until Germany lay in ruins. Everybody was so happy that the war was over at last. People put up flags and banners. At Taunton, the whistles of GWR engines sounded for fifteen minutes across the whole valley at 3.00 pm (VE hour), and thousands gathered on Castle Green to hear Winston Churchill's victory broadcast. At Bridgwater, the dome of the market house was painted red, white and blue. They danced in the streets. Church bells rang. The churches were filled to overflowing. The organist at St Mary Magdalene, Taunton, tells how the people wouldn't go home and stayed till midnight. 'Hitler's body' was taken round in a pram accompanied by 'mourners' and a jazz band. 10,000 people danced in Weston's front and along the streets.

By evening the streets were a solid mass of people both servicemen and civilians. Everyone was most excited and happy. There were street parties in side streets and here and there someone produced an accordion or melodeon and there were singsongs and dancing... the area round the Parade was packed solid and hundreds of people held hands and danced round and round the Parade and Market House and they formed a giant conga line that went completely pound the Parade. The pubs – which had been open all day – had long since sold out and so there was no real drunkenness. It was a spontaneous outburst of sheer joy.

(Eric Saffin)

Mr and Mrs da Costa gave a street party for 60 children in Paradise Square and Duke Street in thanks for the kindness shown them since they were evacuated to the town. Their house was still standing in Bow, London, among all the ruins. Children who grew up in the dark days of the war had never seen such times of enjoyment. Philip Binding was in Vivary Park in Taunton:

The jubilation, dancing, music, fairground attractions and the rest which, together with a fireworks display, went on at Vivary Park was quite something for me and I remember traipsing back home along the Mount Stream path properly exhausted by a whole day of jollifications (children seemed to be on a very 'free to wander' ticket in those days).

VE Day party in a village hall in Minehead. Parties were held all over Britain.

18

The Holocaust

Just as the war was ending the M.P. for Taunton, Colonel E.T.R. Wickham, visited Buchenwald Concentration Camp. As the Allies armies arrived in Germany and saw what evils the Nazis had done to Jews and other people, they wanted members of parliament to come and see the horrors of the concentration camps, so that nobody could say it hadn't happen. Colonel Wickham's hands trembled when he spoke about the cruelty of the Nazi prison guards in these horrible death camps where thousands died. There were even hundreds of children there. They were all 'starving on a basic ration of watery soup of cabbage or turnip and a chunk of bread'.

Frank Foley, born at Highbridge, worked in the British Passport Office in Berlin. Many Jews came to Foley's office for visas to help them escape to Britain. He and his wife also helped hide people in their flat, a dangerous thing to do when they might easily have been caught by the Gestapo (secret police). He even bought train tickets for those who were penniless. Foley worked as a spy for the British through the war, sending information on Nazi plans and movements; he uncovered German spies and used them as double agents. Foley helped to save tens of thousands of Jewish lives. Israel honoured him in 1959 and a grove of pine trees was planted in Israel, each given by a survivor he had helped to rescue from the concentration camps.

After the war Jews who were tough enough to survive went to Palestine and founded the state of Israel.

Frank Foley, working in the British Embassy in Berlin, saved the lives of thousands of Jews who would otherwise have died in the concentration camps.

Dovecot, Forgotten Heroes of Somerset

19
VJ Day

Some towns and villages did not feel it was right to celebrate until the war against Japan was ended. Japan had still not surrendered. Nobody knew how many prisoners were held – and dying – in camps, like Changi Camp, Singapore, with starvation rations. Japanese civilians were starving too. It was not until atomic bombs were dropped that Japan finally surrendered.

War in the Far East ends

8 May 1945	VE Day. The war in Europe ends
6 August 1945	Atomic bomb dropped at Hiroshima
9 August 1945	Atomic bomb dropped at Nagasaki
16 August 1945	VJ Day. The end of war in the East
2 September 1945	Japanese surrender
6-13 October, 1945	Thanksgiving week in Bridgwater

20
After the War – Building a Better World

By the end of the war, everybody and everything was worn out. Soldiers came home and handed in their uniform for new clothes, including a 'demob' suit. There was plenty of work to do repairing buildings. 35,000 homes had been destroyed in Somerset. People thought now they should have a fairer society. They had all worked hard and learnt how to share and how to help each other. In 1945 a Labour government was elected to provide the National Health Service. Poor people could have glasses and go to the dentist free.

FRIENDSHIP BETWEEN COUNTRIES

Many British died in the war:

        264,000 men in services

        35,000 merchant seamen

        60,000 civilians

There was very little food in Germany. Farms were destroyed as armies fought over the fields in 1944-5. Britain had to go on with rationing in order to help feed the Germans in the British zone of Germany. People who lived through the rationing and scarcity even today don't like to see food wasted.

Some Germans came to work in Britain. In the hospital at Cotford.

We saw the first refugees from war-torn Europe... The next batch of foreign labour to arrive at Tone-Vale was German... They were such willing and energetic workers that they soon broke many of the barriers and hatred that the war had naturally left. I was later to find my future wife from among these German recruits.

(Eric Saffin)

Many of the troops who saw the towns of Normandy destroyed wanted to help them. Somerset and Dorset towns became twin towns with them after the war. The Town Twinning movement has given a chance for friendship between the towns of Taunton, Lisieux and Konigslutte. It is planned that Taunton will also be twinned with a town in Poland.

'Prefabs' – houses made from parts pre-fabricated in a factory – in Victory Road, Taunton. They were well designed with built-in kitchens. Each took a day to build.

Glossary & Further Information

ack-ack	anti-aircraft guns, they made a noise like ack-ack
ARP	Air Raid Precautions
called up	have to join the Army, Navy or Airforce
censored	marked out or cut out so that the writing can't be read
demob	demobilisation, leaving the Forces
evacuee	child sent away for safety from towns that might be bombed
Forces	Army, Navy and Airforce
GI	'general' troops from the USA, not the professional soldiers
GWR	Great Western Railway
hush-hush	secret
incendiaries	bombs that catch fire a while after being dropped
Luftwaffe	German for airforce
Overlord	code name for invasion of occupied Europe
pillbox	strong building with slots to shoot from
POW	prisoner of war
prefab	house made with prefabricated (ready-made) parts
RAF	Royal Air Force
Schindler	helped the Jews who worked for him to survive (see the film 'Schindler's List')
segregation	keeping races apart
TB	tuberculosis – a disease
threshing machine	knocks the grain out of the wheat head, ready to grind into flour
U-boats	submarines
US	United States (of America)
WRNS	Women's Royal Naval Service
WVS	Women's Voluntary Service

This is the author in 1939 in a siren suit.

If you want to find out more about the Second World War in Somerset visit:
The Somerset Studies Library, upstairs in Taunton Library (for the largest collection) – 01823 340300
Any public library in Somerset for local information and Internet access – details on www.somerset.gov.uk/libraries
Resources for learning (a subscription service for schools) – 01278 421015
The Military Museum in the Somerset County Museum, Taunton Castle
Somerset County Museum Service, Taunton Castle, Taunton
The Somerset Record Office, Obridge Road, Taunton – appointment necessary 01823 278805
The Fleet Air Arm Museum at Yeovilton
The Tank Museum at Bovington, Dorset
The Imperial War Museum, London
St Fagans, National Museum of Wales, outside Cardiff, has a prefab
Brean Down had gun emplacements
Towns and villages have their own war memorials

Several people who were children in the war have written or recorded their story:
Eric Saffin grew up at Cotford and went to school in Taunton during the war
Philip Binding and his mother came to stay with his grandparents in Taunton
Edward Baverstock was an evacuee in Shapwick
Roy Palmer went to Butleigh to stay away from the bombing in Bristol
Dorothy Evans went to her grandparents in Beckington

Fritz Wolff and John Salvatore were prisoners of war
John Williams was in the Home Guard
Rachel Reckitt went from West Somerset to help the bombed people of Stepney in London; she painted the bombed buildings in London

Syd Durston has recorded his memories of his war time boyhood in water-colour paintings; we are grateful to him for allowing us to use his paintings to bring alive the Somerset countryside as it was in the war time

I am also grateful to Penelope Lively who has allowed me to quote her aunt's (Rachel Reckitt's) adventures in London: you can read about her family in Somerset in her book *A House Unlocked* (Penguin Books, 2002)

Lisieux Museum kindly sent us photographs of their city (Taunton's twin town), so badly damaged in 1944
The Somerset County Gazette is referred to as the *Gazette*